Original title:
Torn Pages

Copyright © 2024 Swan Charm
All rights reserved.

Author: Paulina Pähkel
ISBN HARDBACK: 978-9916-79-150-9
ISBN PAPERBACK: 978-9916-79-151-6
ISBN EBOOK: 978-9916-79-152-3

The Celestial Remnant

In the quiet whispers of night,
Stars dance in the sacred light,
Echoes of the souls above,
Guiding us with endless love.

Ancient tunes the heavens sing,
Joy and peace the angels bring,
A tapestry of grace displayed,
In this world, the lost remade.

Beneath the moon's soft embrace,
Fleeting shadows find their place,
Together we rise from the dust,
In the divine, we put our trust.

Through trials and tribulations clear,
The path unfolds, we draw near,
In faith, we seek the holy flame,
Our hearts ignite, forever the same.

With every prayer, the spirit's flight,
We journey onward—into the light,
In celestial realms, we reunite,
The remnant shines both pure and bright.

Resurrecting the Lost Verses

Whispers from the pages past,
Through time, their echoes last,
Each word a sacred breath,
In the silence, learn from death.

Hidden in the shadows deep,
Ancient verses long to keep,
Resurrected, they softly call,
Inviting us to stand tall.

The ink that flows, a river pure,
Healing hearts, our souls secure,
In each line, a story lives,
In each verse, the spirit gives.

Return to where the lost belong,
In the hymns, we find our song,
A melody of hope and grace,
Resurrecting love in every space.

With open hearts, we find the way,
To honor those who led the sway,
In unity, we hear their voice,
In the sacred, we rejoice.

Lost Verses in Sacred Scrolls

From sacred scrolls, the truth unfolds,
Lost verses wrapped in golden folds,
Each syllable a divine embrace,
In silence, we discover grace.

Ancients spoke in tongues of fire,
Their words igniting our deep desire,
To seek the wisdom they once shared,
In meditations, we prepare.

In the stillness, we unearth,
A treasure trove of holy worth,
Echoes of the time before,
Guiding us to love and more.

As we read these fateful lines,
In every heartbeat, the spirit shines,
Through lost verses, we engage,
And turn anew the sacred page.

In every line, the past resides,
With hope and truth, our hearts collide,
In the scrolls, a journey vast,
Lost verses find their voice at last.

Fragments of the Divine Chronicle

In fragments lie the stories grand,
The divine chronicle at our hand,
Each piece a glimmer of the whole,
A tapestry that speaks to the soul.

Threads of faith woven tight,
Each fragment catching the light,
In the mosaic of time's flight,
We find our way through the night.

The broken pieces beckon near,
With whispered truths for those who hear,
From sorrow blooms the sweetest grace,
In the fragments, we find our place.

Hope arises from the torn,
In the midst of pain, we're reborn,
With every shard, the spirits sing,
In unity, our hearts take wing.

Fragments weaving tales of old,
In their embrace, we break the mold,
Through the divine, we rise anew,
In every piece, the love shines through.

The Lament of withered Scrolls

In sacred chambers lost to time,
The whispers fade, a distant chime.
Ink bleeds softly on the page,
A cry for love from an ancient age.

Beneath the dust, the tales once spoke,
Of faith that soared, and hearts that broke.
The fading light, a solemn grace,
In shadows now, we seek their face.

Oh, scrolls of old, your wisdom wanes,
In silence deep, the spirit gains.
With every turn, a tear unfolds,
In lost Scriptures, a story told.

Yearning souls in their grief repent,
For words of light and hope are sent.
Yet silence here, in echoes swell,
A poignant hymn, a wistful knell.

With every line, a prayer set free,
In holy sorrow, our pleas decree.
The parchment crumbles, yet still I strive,
To find the flame where faith survives.

The Vanished Benedictions

Amidst the ruins of reverent shells,
The echo of prayers, a soft farewell.
Once spoken loud, now barely heard,
In the stillness, our spirits stirred.

The scrolls lie bare, in shadows cast,
Memories of blessings that could not last.
Each whispered hope, like a fading star,
In the night winds, we wander far.

Yet in the void, our hearts still cling,
To sacred words, their gentle ring.
Though time may wane, and shadows loom,
In silent spaces, we find our bloom.

From every crack, the light breaks through,
Illuminating paths for me and you.
In vanished thoughts, benedictions sing,
A chorus sweet of the love they bring.

In sacred chambers, lost yet near,
We gather strength, we cast out fear.
With open hearts, we seek the grace,
Of vanished prayers, in this hallowed space.

Testament of the Wandering Spirit

A spirit roams through valleys wide,
In quest of truth, where shadows bide.
With every step, the ground does quake,
Seeking solace for weary stakes.

In whispered winds, the ancients speak,
Of journeys long, and paths unique.
With head held high, I face the dawn,
In search of love where heart is drawn.

Through arid plains and mountain heights,
A testament of countless flights.
In every breath, the essence yearns,
For wisdom gained and solace earned.

Yet in the still, the darkness waits,
To cloud the mind and seal the fates.
With every trial, the spirit grows,
In wandering faith, it finds repose.

From ancient sages, gifts I glean,
The sacred truths that lie between.
In the wandering, I find my home,
In every soul, no need to roam.

Shattered Prayers

On fractured altars, silence calls,
The splintered hopes, like crumbling walls.
In whispered grief, the angels weep,
For shattered prayers, forever deep.

Each tear that falls, a story penned,
Of faith's endurance, hearts that mend.
Yet in the ruins, blessings hide,
In broken vows, the love abides.

With every crack, the light breaks free,
In fragments, we reclaim our plea.
Unraveled hopes, yet still we stand,
To weave anew with trembling hands.

So gather round, the lost and found,
In shattered dreams, the truth is crowned.
A tapestry of fate and grace,
In every prayer, a sacred trace.

In solemn nights, let courage rise,
As shattered prayers touch the skies.
For in the brokenness, we see,
The beauty of love's mystery.

Elysian Fragments on a Wounded Scroll

In whispers soft, the angels weep,
For sacred truths that time will keep.
Fragments found in shadows cast,
Echoes fading, remnants past.

Beneath the stars, the ancients sigh,
A promise made, beneath the sky.
Healing words from lips once worn,
In silence, souls are gently torn.

The scroll unfolds, yet pages fray,
As light and dark both dance and play.
Elysium calls with voices sweet,
Where broken hearts find soft retreat.

In twilight's grace, the visions bloom,
Amidst the sighs that fill the room.
Revelations in the dusk arrive,
The wounded scroll, where hopes survive.

Oft lost in time, our prayers ascend,
In fragments bound, we seek to mend.
With every breath, our spirits soar,
To find the light, forevermore.

Prayers Inscribed in Broken Time

In moments lost, our voices blend,
With echoes deep that never end.
Prayers written on the winds of fate,
Inscribed in hearts that hope awaits.

The ticking clock, a mournful song,
Where time moves fast, yet feels so wrong.
We seek salvation in shadows cast,
As fleeting dreams, in prayers, are cast.

Through seasons changed, the faith we hold,
In every tear, a story told.
Whispers linger, through night and day,
In broken time, our souls will pray.

The hourglass holds what we can't see,
Faith dances wild, like autumn leaves.
Each grain that falls, a wish confined,
Yet freedom found in love, entwined.

For as we call, our spirits rise,
In fragile hope, we touch the skies.
With every prayer, a thread we weave,
In broken time, we must believe.

The Library of Lost Faith

In dusty tomes, the stories lie,
Of faith once bright, now cast to sky.
Pages yellowed, dreams turn fragile,
In shadows whisper, lost, beguile.

The librarian sits on shelves amassed,
Guarding every truth that fades so fast.
Lost words echo through empty halls,
Each silence speaks as darkness falls.

Retrace the steps where hope once stood,
In every tale, a misunderstood.
The light of wisdom flickers dim,
Yet faithful hearts still long to swim.

Amongst the stacks, we search in vain,
For signs of grace amid the pain.
Each volume thick, a testament
To faith reborn, with hope, content.

We gather dust on weary spines,
Yet still we dream of sacred signs.
In this vast library, we must find,
The threads of faith that bind mankind.

Threads of Eternity in Disarray

In weaving light, the threads of time,
A sacred cloth of reasoned rhyme.
Yet woven loose, our stories fray,
Disarrayed threads, lost on the way.

The loom it creaks, the fabric torn,
As faith and doubt continue worn.
With every stitch, a prayer is spun,
For tangled paths that lead to one.

The tapestry, a vivid dream,
Where colors clash and shadows gleam.
In chaos lived, our spirits dance,
Embracing life, our second chance.

For through the fray, the light will shine,
In broken threads, our hearts align.
A chasm passed, while weaving tight,
We find the thread that leads to light.

Eternity breathes in threads undone,
With every pulse, the journey's won.
In disarray, our spirits sway,
To weave once more, a brand new day.

Revelations of the Unwritten

In shadows deep where whispers dwell,
A truth awaits, no tongue can tell.
The stars above, they weave a tale,
Of silent hope, where dreams prevail.

In sacred spaces, hearts align,
The unseen thread, a path divine.
With prayerful hands, we seek the light,
To guide us through the endless night.

The sacred text, unwritten still,
In every heart, it bends the will.
A promise made, though not in ink,
In quiet moments, we shall think.

Amidst the chaos, peace shall rise,
A gentle touch from ancient skies.
With every heartbeat, find the grace,
In revelations, we embrace.

So walk with faith, through trials bold,
For in each story, love unfolds.
The journey long, yet surely blessed,
In unwritten lines, find soul's rest.

The Frayed Edges of Faith

In frayed edges, our doubts reside,
A tapestry worn, yet full of pride.
With each loose thread, a story brews,
In weariness, we seek the truths.

Through valleys low and mountains high,
The heart whispers, though we may cry.
In moments frail, when strength may wane,
Faith blooms anew, despite the pain.

The hands we grasp, they may let go,
Yet in the shadows, hope does grow.
In sacred whispers, we're not alone,
Together, we find our way back home.

Each frayed edge speaks of journeys past,
Of seeds of love, in silence cast.
With faith renewed, we rise again,
In brokenness, our souls transcend.

Embrace the wear, the threads we bear,
For every tear, a holy prayer.
In frayed edges, grace unfolds,
A testament of hearts so bold.

Echoes in the Fragments

In fragments left, the echoes call,
A soft reminder, we are all.
Each shattered piece, a sacred sign,
Of loss and love, intertwined.

The silent cries of souls set free,
In whispers shared, a mystery.
Through broken paths, we find our way,
In every night, there comes a day.

The fragments glow with inner light,
In patience held, we find the fight.
With open hearts, we seek to mend,
The echoes serve as steps ascend.

Each shattered bond transforms to gold,
In life's embrace, we grow so bold.
When shadows linger, hope will rise,
With echoes clear, we touch the skies.

So cherish all the pieces bright,
In every dark, there shines a light.
For in the fragments, we shall find,
The echoes of the heart and mind.

When Prayers Scatter

When prayers scatter on the breeze,
They float like petals from the trees.
In every heart, a wish unfolds,
A story of the brave and bold.

Each whispered hope, a soft refrain,
In storms of life, we seek the gain.
With every breath, we trust the grace,
In scattered prayers, we find our place.

The heavens hear our silent cries,
Through clouds of doubt, our spirit flies.
In unity, we rise as one,
In scattered prayers, battles won.

The seeds of faith we gently sow,
Through trials faced, we learn and grow.
In every turn, find strength anew,
For scattered prayers will see us through.

So let them soar, those words of love,
In every heart, they rise above.
In scattered prayers, we stand as kin,
For life's true journey, we begin.

The Broken Covenant

In shadows deep where silence dwells,
We mourn the vow that time repels.
The sacred pact, now torn apart,
Whispers of loss in every heart.

The heavens weep, the earth does sigh,
A sacred bond now left to dry.
Forgotten dreams in dust reside,
Where once the faithful did abide.

The altar stands, a shattered stone,
A place once filled with love, now lone.
God's echo fades in distant night,
A flicker lost, devoid of light.

Yet in the ruins, hope is sown,
From broken hearts, new seeds are grown.
We seek the path to find our way,
To mend the bond we lost today.

With every prayer, we lift our plea,
Restore the trust, restore the free.
In faith we stand, though shadows loom,
To gather light from darkest gloom.

Lost Songs of Reverence

In valleys deep where echoes fade,
The songs of praise no longer played.
Our hearts once filled with sweet refrain,
Now whisper low in quiet pain.

The melodies of ages past,
In silence lost, no joy to cast.
We search for harmonies entwined,
In sacred texts, the truth defined.

With every note, a spirit stirred,
Yet now our voices feel unheard.
What once was bright now dims in gray,
The chorus fades, the light gives way.

In longing hearts, the yearning strains,
For songs of hope to break these chains.
We lift our voices high anew,
In reverence, let faith break through.

The lost shall find the song once more,
Reviving echoes on the shore.
With every breath, we sing and soar,
In unity, our spirits roar.

The Ruined Altar

Upon the hill where shadows creep,
The altar lies, a place of sleep.
Once ablaze with fire's light,
Now a memory shrouded in night.

The stones are cracked, the incense lost,
We count the cost of faith's frost.
Once sacred space, now turned to ash,
Time has come, the moments crash.

In silent prayers, the faithful weep,
The blessings buried, secrets keep.
What once was pure, now stained by sin,
A cry for grace to dwell within.

From ruins rise the hearts that seek,
A longing voice, not weak, but meek.
In humility, we gather round,
To forge a hope from broken ground.

With hands held high, we cry aloud,
Restore the altar, make us proud.
In every stone, a promise stands,
In faith united, we take our hands.

Unraveled Sanctity

In sacred halls where whispers roam,
We search for signs to call us home.
The threads of faith begin to fray,
Like morning mist that fades away.

The holy texts now gather dust,
In fragile hands, we place our trust.
What once was clear, now shrouded shade,
A once-bright path in darkness laid.

The candle burns with flickering light,
A beacon lost beyond our sight.
Yet still we hold what once was true,
A yearning heart to break anew.

Against the tide, we raise our song,
In unity, we'll right the wrong.
With every thread, we weave as one,
In sacred love, our work begun.

Reviving hope from sacred ground,
In harmony, our voices sound.
Together we shall find our way,
Restore our faith, come what may.

The Quest for the Lost Testament

In shadows deep, the echoes call,
A journey starts, though frail and small.
With whispers soft, the spirits glide,
Revealing truths that shadows hide.

One step ahead, the heart beats loud,
With faith as shield, I gather shroud.
Through trials fierce, I seek the sign,
A sacred spark, a glimpse divine.

The pages rust, their ink runs thin,
Yet in the dark, the light flows in.
Ancient words, they urge me near,
To understand, to hold what's dear.

And in the quest, I find my way,
Through winding paths where shadows play.
Each moment, grace unfolds its hand,
Revealing what the soul had planned.

So onward still, I tread the line,
Between the lost and the divine.
In every breath, a story lives,
Of testaments and what life gives.

Frayed Lines of Divinity's Path

In the tapestry, threads entwine,
Frayed edges show the grand design.
Wisdom whispers in the breeze,
In stillness found, the heart's at ease.

Each step I take on sacred ground,
A melody of truth resounds.
With every pulse, divinity calls,
Within these lines, the spirit sprawls.

The heavens stretch above my head,
In silence, where the lost have tread.
The path is worn, but I'll persist,
For in the dark, His light exists.

Frayed lines may weave a mighty tale,
Of love unbroken, though we fail.
Through all the storms, the faith stands tall,
In tapestry, I am a part of all.

The journey leads us back to grace,
In every heart, a holy place.
Where frayed lines might seem a test,
Divinity awaits our quest.

Halos in the Abyss of Unwritten Tales

In deep abysses, shadows play,
Yet halos shine, guiding the way.
Unwritten tales, they flicker bright,
In every dark, there's hidden light.

As whispers crawl on silent air,
The souls arise, in prayer they share.
Beyond the void, where silence dwells,
The sacred truth in darkness swells.

Each heartbeat echoes like a drum,
In sacred space, the lost become.
With halos bright, they pierce the night,
In search of tales that spark delight.

The ink may bleed on pages torn,
But in our hearts, the tales are born.
With every breath, a story seeks,
In silence deep, the spirit speaks.

So let the tales begin to weave,
With halos bright, we shall believe.
In every mark, a spark of grace,
In every heart, a holy space.

The Light Pouring from Damaged Pages

From pages worn, the stories flow,
A light that shines, through tears we sow.
In every word, a truth remains,
A guiding spark amidst the chains.

The damaged lines, they whisper low,
Yet in their scars, the wisdom grows.
With every glance, the heart does learn,
From broken things, we find our yearn.

The light pours forth, illuminating,
In every shadow, love translating.
While histories weave a fragile web,
In every message, hope is fed.

So when the pages seem so frail,
In gentle grace, our hearts unveil.
Through all the cracks, a message beams,
Reminding us of larger dreams.

The light persists, it will not fade,
From damaged pages, love is made.
In every tear, a chance to mend,
In every story, we transcend.

The Unseen Hand of Destiny's Pages

In shadows cast by fate's design,
Writings lost, yet still we shine.
A guiding force through dark and light,
The unseen hand, our hearts ignite.

When whispers call from distant shores,
We seek the truth behind closed doors.
Though trials may our spirit shake,
The hand of fate will never break.

Each turn unveils a hidden plot,
In silence dwells a sacred thought.
The pages turn, the ink flows free,
In every line, divinity.

So let us walk with steady grace,
Embrace the path, our rightful place.
For destiny, like rivers flow,
Will lead us where we're meant to go.

In every moment, trust the way,
With faith anew, we greet the day.
For in the book of life we write,
The unseen hand, our guiding light.

Ethereal Words Between the Ruptured Lines

In fragile hearts, the echoes dwell,
Ethereal words, a sacred spell.
They bridge the gaps of time and space,
Where love and loss entwine, embrace.

Through shattered dreams, a message clear,
The whispers ring for all to hear.
Between the lines, a truth resides,
In every wound, the spirit guides.

With gentle grace, the soul will mend,
Each tear a chance for love to blend.
The broken paths, a tapestry,
Of hope and light, our destiny.

So let us seek the divine thread,
In every word, the light we've wed.
Through rupture's pain, we find the whole,
Elysian whispers soothe the soul.

In timeless ink, our stories penned,
The sacred words will never end.
For through the cracks, the light will shine,
Ethereal truth, a gift divine.

Fragments of Faith in the Gale

In tempests fierce, our spirits soar,
Fragments of faith, forevermore.
The winds may howl, the skies may dark,
Yet in our hearts, we find the spark.

Each challenge faced, a lesson learned,
Through trials passed, our souls have burned.
With every gust, we gather strength,
In unity, we walk the length.

So cast away your doubts and fears,
Embrace the light, dry all your tears.
For in the storm, we'll not despair,
With faith as guide, we'll breathe the air.

The gale may rage, but we hold fast,
Through bonds of love, we'll ever last.
In flights of hope, we rise above,
The fragments found, our gift of love.

In every gust, the spirit calls,
With faith we rise, we never fall.
Together strong, our souls unite,
In fragments clear, we find our light.

Beneath the Weight of Unread Scriptures

In dusty tomes, the wisdom sleeps,
Beneath the weight, our silence keeps.
Unread scriptures, sacred, divine,
In pages worn, the truth will shine.

Yet still we seek, with open hearts,
For in the dark, the light imparts.
A yearning deep, the soul's desire,
To read between the lines of fire.

Each verse a path, in shadows laid,
Unraveled dreams by doubt betrayed.
But in the quiet, whispers speak,
Awakening the hearts that seek.

So let us turn those pages old,
Embrace the truths that can't be told.
For in their depths, the light will rise,
Beneath the weight, the soul's surprise.

With fervent prayer, we search anew,
For every line, a promise true.
In unread tomes, the holy grace,
Will guide our hearts to seek His face.

The Struggle for Holy Wholeness

In shadows deep, the heart does roam,
Yearning for light, to find a home.
With faith as guide, we seek the way,
Through trials fierce, we kneel and pray.

Each burden worn, a story told,
A whispered strength, a hand to hold.
In sacred trust, our spirits soar,
In holy wholeness, we are restored.

Sins of the Unsung Chronicles

In quiet nights, the past invades,
With whispered sins, the heart cascades.
Forgotten deeds, they gently sigh,
In silence shared, the soul will cry.

Yet grace abounds, a beacon bright,
In shadows cast, we seek the light.
Redemption's thread, it binds us fast,
In love's embrace, our ghosts are cast.

Revelations Caught in the Wind

The winds of change, they softly call,
Revealing truths that bind us all.
In every breath, a promise sings,
Awakening dreams on gentle wings.

In dawn's first blush, we find our heart,
A sacred bond, we will not part.
The whispers soft, in rustling leaves,
Guide weary souls, as hope believes.

The Fading Light of Transcendent Prose

In pages worn, the stories dwell,
Of sacred truth, and earthly spell.
Each line a prayer, a hymn of grace,
In fading light, we seek a place.

The verses dance, like shadows cast,
Through time and space, their echoes last.
In silent night, we read the lore,
Of love divine, forevermore.

Seraphic Whispers in Shattered Narratives

In shadows deep, the angels sigh,
Their whispers weave through night's soft sky.
A tale untold in broken breath,
Where light and dark dance close to death.

With wings aflame, they guard our dreams,
In every tear, a promise gleams.
The paths we walk, though frail and torn,
Are laid with grace, a hope reborn.

Celestial songs in silence dwell,
Each note a spell, a sacred well.
Through shattered tales, they find their way,
To guide our hearts in night and day.

Echoes rise from ashes lost,
Resilient souls, they bear the cost.
With every prayer, the light grows close,
In shattered narratives, love morose.

So heed the whispers, soft and low,
For in their breath, the answers flow.
Seraphic truths in twilight's gleam,
Awaken faith, ignite the dream.

Echoes of the Unwritten Soul

In the silence of a vacant page,
The whispers of the heart engage.
A truth unturned in shadows cast,
Holds echoes of a love amassed.

Like rivers flow through barren land,
The soul unveils a guiding hand.
Each heartbeat knows the untold grace,
In quietude, we seek our place.

Beneath the stars, a story brews,
With every tear, the heavens fuse.
The ink of pain, the quill of joy,
In silent moments, we deploy.

Unwritten hymns in twilight air,
Imbued with dreams and sacred care.
Through whispered prayers, we find our way,
In echoes where our spirits play.

So listen close, the truths unfold,
In every glance, the heart is bold.
An unwritten song, divine and whole,
Awaits the dawn of every soul.

Celestial Gaps in Holy Text

In sacred lines, the ink will fade,
Yet truth remains in shadows laid.
Within the gaps, the light transcends,
A glimpse of grace that never ends.

The holy whispers call our name,
In every heart, a spark of flame.
Through ancient texts, we seek the new,
In celestial gaps, our spirits grew.

With faith we tread where few have gone,
In every void, we find a song.
The lessons learned from silence wide,
Guide weary hearts with love inside.

Beneath the stars, a promise gleams,
In every gap, the hope redeems.
Through sacred voids, the soul finds peace,
A melody that shall not cease.

So listen well, for wisdom's call,
In celestial gaps, we rise and fall.
Our hearts align with every breath,
In holy text, beyond all death.

Spiritual Echoes in Faded Scripts

In faded scripts, the voices sway,
Their truths concealed in shades of gray.
Each passage speaks of love and loss,
A journey marked by cross and dross.

With ancient words, the spirits weave,
A tapestry for us to cleave.
Through echoes soft, we find our way,
In whispered prayers, we humbly pray.

The scriptures hold the tales of yore,
Of battles fought and hearts that soar.
In every line, the sacred art,
Reflects the light that fills the heart.

Within the pages, wisdom blooms,
In every shadow, hope resumes.
Though faded now, the truths remain,
A spark of faith amidst the pain.

So heed the whispers from the past,
In faded scripts, love's shadows cast.
For in their depths, we find our role,
Spiritual echoes that mend the soul.

Shards of the Divine

In the stillness of the night,
Whispers of angels take flight.
Light gleams on fractured glass,
Reflections of the holy pass.

Glimmers dance in sacred air,
Every shard a breath of prayer.
Fragments of truth, glistening bright,
A mosaic of faith, pure light.

From the darkness comes the gleam,
Faith ignites a fervent dream.
Every piece tells a story,
In each shard, a hint of glory.

Hearts unite, come and see,
The beauty of divinity.
In brokenness, we find the whole,
A testament to the soul.

Gathered under the vast sky,
In the quiet, spirits fly.
Hand in hand, we reach above,
In the shards, we find our love.

The Silenced Testament

In shadows deep, the voice retreats,
A silence swells where hope still beats.
Each verse unsaid, a heart's lament,
In voiceless realms, the truth is spent.

Pages tattered, ink runs dry,
Echoes linger, questioning why.
Chapters lost to the tempest's toll,
Yet still they seek the sacred scroll.

Beneath the surface, a rhythm flows,
In quiet moments, the spirit knows.
Though silence reigns, the heart will sing,
In stillness, the soul takes wing.

Hope flickers in the fading light,
Silent prayers ascend to night.
Amidst the chaos, peace may bloom,
In the void, arises room.

Towards the dawn, we turn our gaze,
To find the voice within the haze.
For in the silence, truth does dwell,
A hidden tale, a sacred swell.

Scriptures in Disarray

Lost among the crumpled lines,
Hopes entwined with ancient signs.
Pages flutter like restless wings,
Between the chaos, wisdom sings.

Fragments scattered, tales untold,
In the margins, dreams unfold.
Writing seeks to find its path,
In scribbled notes, we feel the wrath.

Beneath the surface, meaning hides,
In labyrinthine thoughts, it bides.
Every story, a puzzle's thread,
In the mess, divine is spread.

Yet through the turmoil, light breaks free,
Revealing truths that long to be.
In disarray, a sacred call,
To gather hope from shadow's fall.

Through the clutter, hearts align,
Finding solace in the divine.
For in the chaos, love can grow,
A testament to what we know.

Ink on the Wind

Words drift softly on the breeze,
Carried forth with whispered ease.
In the air, each phrase alights,
A message born of sacred heights.

Beneath the stars, they weave and sway,
Ink on the wind, night turns to day.
Stories written in the sky,
With every gust, we hear the why.

Echoes of prayers, they swirl and spin,
A chorus of grace that draws us in.
In every flutter, a heart's delight,
Illuminating the endless night.

As we listen to the quiet throng,
The universe hums a timeless song.
Ink on the wind, a transient gift,
In its gentle flow, our spirits lift.

So let the winds of fate declare,
The sacred truths beyond compare.
With every breath, we find our part,
Ink on the wind, the voice of the heart.

Celestial Fragments Adrift

In the quiet of the night, they shine,
Stars of mercy that intertwine.
Whispers of love, soft and clear,
Guiding hearts through doubt and fear.

Lost in the fabric of divine grace,
Each spark a map, a holy place.
Endless journey, souls in flight,
United in hope, forever bright.

Fragments of dreams scattered wide,
Yet in the shadows, angels glide.
Celestial truths that never fade,
In the light of faith, they cascade.

The heavens hum a sacred tune,
Carried gently, like a swoon.
Galaxies dance, a cosmic blend,
In this embrace, our spirits mend.

Shattered pieces, a wondrous whole,
A tapestry woven by the soul.
Each strand a prayer, a silent vow,
To the infinite, we humbly bow.

Echoes of Unwritten Prophecy

In the stillness, whispers rise,
Echoes from beyond the skies.
Unwritten tales of heart and mind,
In sacred pages, truth we find.

The past resounds with lessons learned,
In silence, the fire is burned.
Futures await with bated breath,
In every moment, we dance with death.

Seek the light within the dark,
Each flicker ignites a spark.
Voices of the lost and found,
In the harmony, we are bound.

Prophecies whispered through the breeze,
Nature's secrets, the soul's keys.
Listen closely, and you'll see,
The tapestry of destiny.

In currents deep, our spirits swim,
Navigating shadows, on a whim.
In this quest, we intertwine,
Echoes of truth, forever shine.

Signs of Surrendered Truth

In the heart where shadows play,
Surrender whispers, come what may.
Signs appear on paths we tread,
Each step a promise, gently said.

The weight of burdens fades away,
As we embrace the light of day.
In letting go, we find our wings,
The joy that surrendering brings.

Truth unveiled in simple grace,
A mirror held to all we face.
In each moment, a lesson laid,
With every tear, a blessing made.

Softly spoken truths ignite,
In the darkness, love's pure light.
The soul awakens, free and bold,
In every heartbeat, stories told.

Surrender thus becomes our creed,
In every action, thought, and deed.
With open arms, we learn to trust,
In this divine dance, we must.

Sacred Remnants of the Soul

In the ashes of what once was,
Lies the spark of sacred cause.
Remnants glow with ancient fire,
Lit by hope, our hearts aspire.

Through trials fierce, the spirit grows,
A garden blooms through winter's snows.
The soul's essence, pure and bright,
Guided by an inner light.

In the silence, hear the call,
Wisdom found in every fall.
Each fragment sings a sacred song,
In unity, we all belong.

Threads of fate entwine and weave,
In every breath, we learn to believe.
The journey crafted, step by step,
In this vast dance, we find our depth.

With open hearts, we seek, we yearn,
In every lesson, a chance to learn.
For in the remnants, beauty thrives,
A testament that love survives.

Wandering Glimpses of Grace

In fields where shadows play,
We seek the light that stays.
Grace whispers through the trees,
In every gentle breeze.

Hearts open like the sky,
To wonders passing by.
Each moment, softly spun,
Reflects the light of One.

Through valleys dark and deep,
We find the soul's true keep.
A flicker, just a sign,
Of love that intertwines.

In silence we can hear,
The heavens drawing near.
Every step we take with trust,
Transforms our fear to dust.

With purpose as our guide,
In faith, we safely bide.
Wandering, we embrace,
The endless glimpse of grace.

Broken Chains of Faith

Once bound by heavy sorrow,
We clasp a brighter tomorrow.
Chains that held us tight,
Now shattered in the light.

Through trials we have grown,
In unity, not alone.
Fingers raised in prayer,
Our burdens laid right there.

Hope emerges from the pain,
A promise will remain.
Faith ignited, never dim,
In shadows, He is hymn.

Together we shall rise,
To see beyond the skies.
With hearts no longer bound,
In freedom, love resounds.

Each breath a song of peace,
From struggle, sweet release.
With broken chains we stand,
In grace, we join His hand.

The Echoes of Forgotten Voices

In whispers of the past,
Where echoes seem to last.
Voices calling us to stand,
In faith, a guiding hand.

Through shadows thick and long,
Resound the ancient song.
Teachings from days of yore,
Still linger on the shore.

Winds carry tales of grace,
Time cannot erase.
Lessons written in the heart,
A sacred work of art.

In the quiet, we find strength,
As we journey forth in length.
With wisdom of the sage,
We turn another page.

United with the lost,
In remembrance, we are embossed.
Echoes guide us through the strife,
In shadows, we find life.

Threads of a Divine Narrative

In fabric woven fine,
Each thread a tale divine.
Stories told through time,
In rhythm, prayer, and rhyme.

Stitched with love and grace,
We find our rightful place.
Patterns in the night sky,
A promise draws us nigh.

In every joy and tear,
The sacred draws us near.
Together we are spun,
In truth, we are made one.

Each challenge faced with trust,
Reveals what's pure and just.
With threads of light and shade,
The universe displayed.

As we walk this path so wide,
In faith, we shall abide.
Every heart a part,
Of this divine art.

The Fractured Choir

In sacred halls where echoes wane,
A melody lost, yet hearts remain.
Voices once pure, now drift apart,
Seeking the light, yearning to start.

The notes of faith, in disarray,
Whispers of hope, in shadows play.
Each soul a thread, a different hue,
Together forming a tapestry true.

Through trials faced and burdens borne,
The choir stands firm, though souls are worn.
Each fractured voice, a story told,
In harmony's grasp, love will unfold.

From silence grows a gentle prayer,
A sacred bond, beyond compare.
In unity, we find our way,
To weave the night into the day.

Together still, though lost we seem,
A fractured choir, yet one in dream.
With every flaw, a strength we share,
In love's embrace, we find repair.

Disjoined Chants of Silence

In shadows deep, where spirits weep,
Disjoined chants fall, a promise to keep.
The silence echoes, a haunting song,
In whispers soft, we seek where we belong.

With every breath, a prayer ascends,
A silent plea that never ends.
Amidst the void, our hearts ignite,
In the stillness, we find our light.

Each fragment lost, in time's cruel hand,
Yearns for the touch of a sacred land.
In the quiet, our souls align,
In disjoined chants, the truth will shine.

Through trials faced and shadows cast,
We rise together, to break the fast.
The sacred pulse, within us thrives,
In joined silence, a hymn arrives.

With every note, our spirits soar,
In disjoined chants, we seek for more.
The silence sings, a lullaby sweet,
In harmony's fold, our hearts repeat.

Wrapped in the Shadows of Reverie

In dreams we wander, souls entwined,
Wrapped in shadows, seeking the divine.
Visions whisper of a brighter day,
In reverie's grip, we find our way.

The stars above, like diamonds glow,
Guiding our paths where we yearn to go.
In silent prayer, our hopes take flight,
Wrapped in shadows, we ignite the night.

Each thought a spark, a candle's flame,
In darkness deep, we call His name.
Wrapped in the love of the unseen,
Through shadows cast, our faith will glean.

In reverie's realm, our spirits rise,
Touched by grace, beneath sprawling skies.
With every heartbeat, a whisper clear,
In shadows' embrace, we've nothing to fear.

Through twilight vale, the dawn will break,
In reverie wrapped, our souls awake.
With hearts aligned, we dance as one,
In shadows of faith, our journey's begun.

The Ever-Distant Covenant

A promise made, yet far away,
In hearts we hold what words can't say.
The ever-distant covenant calls,
In sacred whispers, love enthralls.

Through trials endured, we stand alone,
Each step we take, a seed that's sown.
The threads of fate, so finely spun,
In every challenge, our hearts will run.

With grace bestowed, we seek the path,
To find the joy within the wrath.
Though distant now, the bond remains,
In every struggle, love sustains.

A beacon bright, amidst the night,
The solemn vow, our guiding light.
In every heartbeat, every prayer,
The ever-distant, love laid bare.

Together still, though miles may part,
In every sigh, we'll find the start.
For in our souls, a truth will hold,
The ever-distant covenant, told.

The Tapestry of Sacred Ruins

In shadows cast by ancient stones,
Whispers of the past still moan.
A tapestry of faith and loss,
Threads of sorrow, love embossed.

Ruins speak, yet silence holds,
Stories lost, now centuries old.
Artistry of hands now dust,
Yet in the ruins, hearts still trust.

Beneath the arch of crumbling light,
Echoes linger in the night.
Beacons dim, yet flickers reign,
Eternal hope amidst the pain.

Each fragment bears a heaven's seal,
Life and death, a sacred wheel.
In every crack, divinity,
A glimpse of what there used to be.

So wander we through sacred sites,
Seeking solace, finding lights.
In the ruins, our spirits sing,
For every ending births new spring.

Eternal Questions in Fragmented Phrases

What is truth, a fleeting dream?
In shadows cast, we hear the theme.
Silent echoes, thoughts collide,
In whispered prayers, our souls abide.

Who am I in this vast expanse?
A fleeting thought, a wisp, a dance.
Seeking meaning in every breath,
Chasing light amidst the death.

Why must love falter, fade away?
In aching hearts, we long to stay.
Questions linger like stars at sea,
Fracted phrases, our destiny.

When will peace embrace the world?
In strife, the banners are unfurled.
Yet, in the chaos, hope resides,
In torn fibers, grace abides.

How does faith weave through despair?
In whispered truths, we find a prayer.
Eternal questions, though unchained,
In every heart, love's written name.

Ethereal Insights of the Unseen

Beyond the veil of worldly sight,
Lies a realm of purest light.
Ethereal whispers float like dreams,
In the silence, divine essence beams.

Glimpses of grace in every breath,
Life transcends both joy and death.
In twilight's hue, the spirit flies,
Revealing truths beyond the skies.

What lies beyond the mortal coil?
In sacred grounds, does faith unsoil?
The unseen world calls out with grace,
Beyond the heart, it's our embrace.

In the stillness of a sacred hour,
Mysteries bloom, a fragrant flower.
Awakening thoughts, minds align,
In ethereal realms, stars entwine.

With eyes shut tight, we seek to find,
The threads that link all humankind.
Ethereal insights softly blend,
In love, we find the truths ascend.

Spiritual Parchments Singed by Time

Pages worn with age and grace,
Stories etched in every space.
Spiritual whispers inked in dust,
Faith and wisdom, ever thrust.

Through burning fires, the text remains,
Lessons learned through joy and pains.
Each parchment holds a tale of soul,
In sacred rhythms, we feel whole.

The lessons of the hearts entwined,
In every passage, peace we find.
Words may fade, yet truths endure,
In every crease, there lies a cure.

From ashes rise the tales of yore,
In every line, a world to explore.
Singed by time, yet holy still,
A map to guide the wandering will.

So let us read each faded scroll,
With open hearts and softened soul.
For timeless wisdom guides our way,
In spiritual parchment, night and day.

The Mended Heart of Lost Worship

In silence the whispers of prayers breathe,
Hearts once shattered seek solace in light.
The echoes of faith guide the weary souls,
Mended by grace, they rise to the night.

From ashes of doubt, springs forth a new song,
With every tear shed, the spirit finds peace.
The altar of hope, rebuilt from despair,
Embracing the love that shall never cease.

Hands clasped in reverence, we gather once more,
In unity bound, through trials we grow.
The light of the sacred ignites in our hearts,
And kindles the fire of all we bestow.

As shadows of worldly temptations may loom,
We walk on the paths that the prophets have laid.
In the garden of mercy, our faith blooms anew,
The mended heart sings of the love unafraid.

So let us be vessels of truth and of grace,
For every lost moment may still be restored.
In the tapestry woven, we find our own place,
In the mended heart whispers of worship adored.

In the Ashes of the Profound

In the shadows of silence, wisdom prevails,
From ashes of sorrow, a flame flickers bright.
The remnants of yearning converge in the dusk,
And beckon the lost to the chorus of light.

In the depths of despair, a seed softly grows,
Roots tethered in faith, reaching high to the skies.
Through trials and tears, all burdens transform,
As hearts once forlorn lift their gaze, rise and rise.

The embers of pain illuminate the way,
In the desert of doubt, a river flows free.
The sacred unfolds in mysterious forms,
Initiating souls to the vastness of sea.

So speak to the heart that seeks knowledge of grace,
Embrace every moment, each breath that we take.
In the canvas of time, our colors collide,
In the ashes of profound, our spirits awake.

Brave souls walk the path that is written in stars,
In the whispers of night, the old and the new.
We rise from the embers, renewed, unconfined,
In the ashes of the profound, we find what is true.

The Divergent Path of Faith

In twilight we gather, where choices unfold,
The winds of belief guide our steps along way.
With courage our lanterns illuminate dark,
On the divergent path, we trust and we sway.

Each moment a whisper, each trial a test,
The echoes of love, they call like a song.
In uncertainty's arms, we find strength anew,
Embracing the journey, where all souls belong.

With hearts intertwined, we gather our dreams,
The tapestry woven with threads of the brave.
Through valleys of fear, we stand hand in hand,
Refuge in faith, we bring light to the grave.

Mountains may tremble, and rivers may roar,
Yet solid we stand, as the ground turns to stone.
With purpose we traverse the pathways of fate,
In the diverging road, we never walk alone.

So let us take solace in questing our truth,
In the mosaic of life, the varied collide.
For in every divergent path we embrace,
The sacred connection in which we abide.

Sacred Whispers in Ruins

In sacred ruins where memories dwell,
The stories of ancients linger and weave.
Soft whispers of wisdom breathe life into stone,
Through echoes of time, our spirits believe.

The arches of faith rise like bridges of light,
Guiding the lost, where shadow meets grace.
In the stillness of twilight, the heart finds its path,
Through sacred whispers, a holy embrace.

From brokenness springs a garden of hope,
In the soil of burdens, new blooms appear.
With every lost prayer, redemption draws near,
In ruins transformed, the divine whispers clear.

The tapestry stitched with threads of the past,
Reminds us of journeys that shaped who we are.
In the sacred remnants, a beauty unfolds,
In ruins we find our most luminous star.

So gather around the remnants of grace,
Each stone tells a story of trials embraced.
For in sacred whispers, we rise and we seek,
In the ruins of love, our spirits find space.

Vestiges of Grace in the Fall

In autumn's embrace, leaves drift and sway,
Whispering prayers at the end of the day.
Grace in decay, in hues of deep gold,
Stories of mercy in whispers retold.

Beneath the branches, shadows do dance,
Lost in reflection, in quiet romance.
A promise of hope in the chill of the air,
Life finds a way in the heart of despair.

Crimson and amber, a tapestry bright,
Each leaf a lesson in fading light.
Nature's own hymn, a seraphic call,
A testament whispered, 'Grace conquers all.'

From roots that are hallowed, new life shall sprout,
Emerging from layers of fall's soft doubt.
The cycle continues, a divine decree,
In vestiges scattered, God's love we can see.

So gather your heart in this sacred space,
Amidst all the changes, unfold His grace.
Though seasons may shift, and shadows may fall,
In vestiges of hope, we hear His soft call.

Notes from an Abandoned Sanctuary

Once hallowed hall, now whispers remain,
Echoes of prayers, like soft falling rain.
Dust on the pews, yet spirits still soar,
Carrying hopes from that old wooden door.

Sunlight filters through windows of glass,
Casting soft shadows where memories pass.
Each note in the silence, a deep, sacred sigh,
Bearing witness to faith that will never die.

The altar stands still, adorned with old scars,
Each mark a reminder of reaching for stars.
The faded hymnals tell stories untold,
Of love and redemption in pages of gold.

In corners of anguish, a flicker of light,
Rekindling warmth through the chill of the night.
The sanctuary's breath, a prayer yet unsung,
In echoes of hope, forever it's strung.

So linger awhile in this sacred retreat,
Where memories linger and lost hearts may meet.
In the silence of shadows, find solace, find peace,
In notes ever written, may our burdens cease.

The Quiet Chaos of Sacred Essays

In quiet moments, truth gently unfolds,
Words woven softly, like threads into gold.
Essays of spirit in ink that is pure,
Chasing the shadows, embracing the obscure.

The chaos of life in passion laid bare,
Each line a reflection, a sacred prayer.
Thoughts intertwine with the breath of the Divine,
Seeking the solace where hearts intertwine.

In the margins, wisdom, though hidden, is found,
Whispers of angels, an ethereal sound.
The tumult of living, a canvas of grace,
Every sacred struggle a step in this race.

Pondering moments where faith seems to wane,
The chaos of life, a chance to reclaim.
A tapestry woven with threads of our pain,
Find beauty in chaos, let love be our gain.

So write down your heart, let the chaos be seen,
In essays of spirit, let all intervene.
For within every struggle, a lesson is sown,
In quietest chaos, our souls are revealed.

Remnants of Hope in Faded Ink

On pages once vibrant, now yellowed and frail,
Lie remnants of stories that time could not pale.
Faded ink whispers the dreams that we chased,
In the heart of the author, each moment embraced.

Through trials and triumphs, the spirit remained,
In writings of hope, where love has been gained.
Each letter a testament, a reflection of grace,
In the remnants of ink, we find our true place.

The quill now rests softly, but words never die,
In the silence of pages, the echoes still cry.
For struggles ignited, and passions entwined,
Breathe life into the heart when the soul feels resigned.

In time's gentle passage, our stories are told,
Remnants of hope in the shadows of old.
Turn softly the pages, let each word resound,
In the dance of our dreams, we are glory-bound.

So cherish the ink in the corners of mind,
For hope in each letter is waiting to find.
In the remnants of history, our spirit will rise,
In faded ink solace, our purpose lies.

Revelations Interrupted by Time's Hand

In shadows cast by fleeting days,
The truth eludes in quiet ways.
We search for signs on battered ground,
Yet silence is the only sound.

Time's hand upon our weary brow,
Calls forth the past, yet leaves us low.
Each moment lost, a fleeting ghost,
In whispers, we learn what matters most.

The sacred texts in fragments tell,
Of hope that blooms from grief's dark well.
Yet faith, though riven, still dreams bright,
Guided by a hidden light.

The heavens weep for paths untried,
While hearts in prayer, with love abide.
Through trials, we are forged anew,
In pain, the gentle spirit grew.

Like stars that pierce the velvet night,
Our doubts remain, yet faith takes flight.
For in the dark, a spark will gleam,
And in our souls, a sacred dream.

The Pilgrim's Guide to Shattered Belief

Upon the road, the weary tread,
With burdens borne and dreams unsaid.
Each step, a prayer, a mournful cry,
For truths that fade, yet will not die.

The compass spins, the way unclear,
Yet love, relentless, draws us near.
In chaos, we seek ancient grace,
Through shattered beliefs, we find our place.

With every stone that marks our way,
We gather faith like seeds of day.
In gardens wild, the spirit grows,
Through tempests fierce and quiet prose.

The heart is both a sword and shield,
In fractured lands, our fate is sealed.
Yet hope can rise, as dawn ascends,
In every ending, grace transcends.

We walk in shadows, side by side,
As pilgrims on a faith-filled ride.
In every doubt, a glimpse of light,
Together, we embrace the night.

From ashes, we shall surely rise,
In unity, our spirits fly.
Through shattered beliefs, we mend the thread,
In love's embrace, we're gently led.

Serene Echoes Between the Fractured Texts

In ink and dust, the pages sigh,
Amidst the chaos, we wonder why.
The echoes call from ancient lines,
As sacred whispers intertwine.

Beneath the weight of questions deep,
The soul's unrest will never sleep.
We hold the shards of what was said,
In every word, the spirit's thread.

Through fractured texts, the truths unfold,
With each reveal, the heart grows bold.
In silence wrapped, the wisdom lies,
A timeless gift, a child's surprise.

The melody of faith is sung,
In lives of saints, the prophets sprung.
With every loss, a chance to find,
The grace that rests in love entwined.

Across the realms of heart and mind,
We seek the peace that's hard to find.
In every tear, a sacred time,
To glimpse the love, to taste the sublime.

So gather 'round the hearth of trust,
In fractured texts, our hearts adjust.
With every echo, we draw near,
In unity, we shed our fear.

Psalms Whispers Beneath the Fractured Veil

In twilight's hush, the whispers flow,
Beneath the veil, the ancients know.
Each psalm we sing, a sacred breath,
In life's embrace, beyond the death.

With every tear, a prayer descends,
The heartache fades; the spirit bends.
In shadows deep, where sorrow dwells,
A song is born, a tale it tells.

Through veils of doubt and threads of pain,
In every loss, there's love to gain.
The soul connects in sacred space,
A tapestry of time and grace.

So lift your voice to skies above,
In fractured hymns, we'll find our love.
Through trials faced, our hearts will soar,
As psalms whisper forevermore.

In gentle light, the truth appears,
Beyond the veil, we'll cast our fears.
In every breath, a promise bright,
We walk as one, into the light.

Shattered Testaments of Faith

In shadows deep, the truth is sought,
A journey fraught with battles fought.
Each broken vow, a lesson learned,
In fiery trials, our spirits burned.

Yet through the cracks, a light will shine,
A holy grace, a love divine.
With every tear, we find our way,
In shattered faith, we rise to pray.

Hands lifted high, we seek the skies,
With whispered hopes and silent sighs.
In every heart, the flame ignites,
As shattered testaments bring new sights.

Together bound, in spirit's flight,
We walk the path, embracing night.
Belief may wane, but still we stand,
With faith as strong as shifting sand.

In weary souls, our trust remains,
In shattered testaments, love sustains.
We forge anew, from loss and pain,
In every heart, a faith reclaimed.

Scattered Leaves of Revelation

In autumn's breath, the leaves descend,
Each whisper holds a tale to send.
From ancient trees, the words unfold,
Scattered leaves of wisdom old.

Upon the ground, they rustle low,
A gentle heart, where insights flow.
In twilight's glow, we find our way,
As scattered leaves invite to pray.

The season turns, the cycle spins,
In every end, a new begins.
With open eyes, we seek the truth,
In scattered leaves, our aching youth.

A sacred touch in every hue,
Reminders of the love that's true.
In letting go, we find our peace,
As scattered leaves grant soul's release.

From past to present, lessons weave,
In whispered winds, we learn to believe.
With hope reborn, we rise anew,
In scattered leaves, our spirits grew.

The Whisper of Ancient Psalms

In twilight's hush, the verses bloom,
Echoed softly through the gloom.
Ancient psalms, a sacred breath,
In whispered tones, we conquer death.

With every line, a promise made,
In faith's embrace, our fears do fade.
The hymns of old, forever sing,
In quiet nights, our souls take wing.

Through trials faced and shadows cast,
The whispers of the ages last.
With every prayer, unbroken chain,
The ancient psalms, our hearts remain.

In moments lost, they softly call,
A guiding hand through rise and fall.
The rhythm beats in time with grace,
In ancient psalms, we find our place.

Together we soar, our spirits high,
With whispered truth, we touch the sky.
In harmony, our voices blend,
The whisper of psalms, life's truest friend.

Frayed Edges of Belief

In paged tomes where stories fade,
Frayed edges speak of faith displayed.
With tender hands, we turn the leaves,
In every line, the heart believes.

The memories weave in shadows light,
In frayed edges, we claim the night.
A tapestry of love and grace,
In every fray, a sacred space.

Through trials felt, the rips we mend,
In faith's embrace, we find our friend.
With every prayer, the healing flows,
In frayed edges, our spirit grows.

The journey marked by scars and strife,
In frayed edges, we find our life.
A testament to battles won,
In faith's embrace, we are as one.

As years unfold, the pages turn,
In frayed edges, our hearts still yearn.
Together bound, we rise and stand,
In frayed edges, we hold His hand.

The Sanctity of Unwritten Prayers

In the quiet of the night,
Whispers rise like misty light.
Hearts speak deep, their secrets bare,
Faithful souls in silent prayer.

Angels gather, none can see,
Listening close, as love runs free.
Each thought a beam, a sacred fire,
Holding dreams, lifting them higher.

Moments pass, yet time stands still,
In the silence, a holy thrill.
The world outside may drift away,
But here, in stillness, we shall stay.

Grains of faith, like stars they shine,
Unseen grace in each design.
Woven threads of hope and care,
In the stillness, prayers laid bare.

Eternity in a breath we find,
The heart's embrace, forever kind.
In unwritten words, we trust and sway,
The sanctity of prayer's ballet.

Dispersing the Sacred Dust

From ancient stones, a tale unfolds,
Of sacred dreams and whispers told.
Upon the winds, the echoes glide,
Dispersing dust where angels bide.

In the forest, light doth weave,
A tapestry for hearts to cleave.
Beneath the boughs, the spirit stirs,
In rustling leaves, the voice of hers.

Every grain, a memory holds,
Of love once shared and stories bold.
The sacred dust, a bridge to grace,
Binding the lost, a warm embrace.

Through aching skies and trembling earth,
Awakened lives shout songs of birth.
In fragile hands, we sow and trust,
Fate mingles here with sacred dust.

Glory found in humble places,
In every smile, each spirit traces.
Together we rise, a joyful surge,
Dispelling doubts as souls emerge.

The Silent Scribes of Heaven

In shadows where the twilight falls,
Heaven's scribes pen sacred calls.
With ink of stars and whispered grace,
They capture all in this hallowed space.

Every tear, a word of love,
Every sigh, a prayer above.
Silent witnesses to our plight,
Their quills aglow with holy light.

In the stillness, stories weave,
Threads of joy, of loss, believe.
Each moment writes upon the skies,
As all our dreams begin to rise.

With tender hands, they shape our fate,
In parchment skies, they patiently wait.
For when we doubt and seek to stray,
These scribes will guide us on our way.

Thus, let our hearts in faith abide,
With trust, we lean upon their side.
For in the silence, they bestow,
The love and light that we all know.

Eclipsed by Time's Embrace

As day gives way to night's embrace,
The stars emerge, a timeless grace.
In cosmic dance, they gently play,
Whispers of souls that lost their way.

In shadow's cast, our fears take flight,
Yet hope glimmers through velvet night.
Each heartbeat counts the moments passed,
Eclipsed by time, yet love will last.

Guided by faith's enduring flame,
We seek the path, we seek the name.
Within the storm, a shelter found,
For in our hearts, grace shall abound.

Memories of the past reside,
Carried forth on the evening tide.
Each echo sings, a calling clear,
Eclipsed by time, yet always near.

Breathe deep the truth, let courage sway,
In every dawn, the shadows play.
For love transcends what time's embraced,
And in our hearts, it finds its place.

Undaunted Hearts Amidst the Fragments

In fragments scattered, faith still glows,
Hearts undaunted face the silent woes.
Through shattered dreams, a whisper calls,
In every ruin, the spirit stands tall.

Hope like embers, ignites the night,
Guiding lost souls towards the light.
Each piece of sorrow, a lesson learned,
In brokenness, a fire burns.

With courage spanning across the vast,
We mend our wounds, forget the past.
In unity, we find our voice,
In faith's embrace, we still rejoice.

Mountains may crumble, oceans rise,
Yet undaunted hearts will reach the skies.
For in each trial, a blessing shows,
A tapestry rich, that only love knows.

So stand together, hand in hand,
In the midst of ruins, we boldly stand.
With undaunted hearts, we'll play our part,
Reviving hope in every heart.

A Pilgrim's Journey Amidst the Ruins

A pilgrim walks through ancient stone,
Seeking solace, never alone.
Each step echoes the past's long tale,
In ruins found, the spirit shall sail.

Beneath the shadows of time's embrace,
Hope survives in this sacred space.
With every whisper of the wandering breeze,
The heart remembers, the soul finds peace.

Through fields of sorrow, seeds of grace,
In every heart, a sacred place.
Though the path may be rugged and dire,
Faith ignites a perpetual fire.

On roads less traveled, wisdom grows,
In each encounter, the spirit knows.
The ruins speak, as the pilgrim learns,
Through trials faced, the soul returns.

So onward marches the faithful few,
In every ruin, a world anew.
With gratitude, they sing their song,
A journey shared, where all belong.

Divine Dust on Forgotten Leaves

Amidst the branches, whispers play,
Divine dust glimmers, soft as day.
Forgotten leaves tell stories grand,
In silent praise, they humbly stand.

Bathed in twilight, where shadows dance,
Spirit dances in sacred trance.
Each leaf holds a moment lost,
In nature's arms, we count the cost.

From seeds of faith, new life shall rise,
In the depths of despair, hope can surprise.
Divine dust falls like gentle rain,
Hearts reborn from sorrow's pain.

So pause and listen in sacred groves,
In nature's heart, the spirit roves.
With every breath, the world unfolds,
As divine whispers breathe the bold.

In quiet corners, grace appears,
Infusing life with love, not fears.
On forgotten leaves, we find our peace,
In unity's warmth, our hearts release.

The Light Beyond the Shredded Glyphs

In ancient scripts, the truth resides,
Yet shredded glyphs, the heart still guides.
Through wild chaos, a spark remains,
A light that dances, breaks the chains.

Though words may fail, and vision fade,
The spirit's song cannot evade.
In silent prayer, a beacon glows,
In every heart, the light bestows.

Across the ages, wisdom speaks,
In whispered truths the spirit seeks.
The tangled paths may cloud the view,
Yet faith reveals what's pure and true.

From shadows cast, we rise anew,
With courage strong, we seek what's due.
For beneath the wreckage, hope resides,
In every heart, the spirit guides.

To journey forth with open eyes,
To find the light that never dies.
Beyond the glyphs, a promise gleams,
In love's embrace, we share our dreams.

Reverent Shadows on Dusty Pages

In quiet hour, the pages turn,
Whispers of faith through shadows burn.
Each word a light, soft and divine,
Guiding the soul, in grace we entwine.

Stories of old, in silence dwell,
Echoes of truth, in heart they swell.
Beneath the dust, a promise lies,
Awakening hope, where spirit flies.

The ink of ages, a sacred thread,
Binding the living with those who've fled.
In solemn prayer, we read their signs,
In reverent shadows, our fate aligns.

Lost in the scrolls, our burdens laid,
In solemn whispers, the debt is paid.
The light of wisdom, a guiding star,
Illuminates paths, both near and far.

As every dusk must yield to dawn,
So all must rise, though ages gone.
With every heartbeat, the truth remains,
Reverent shadows, where love sustains.

Pilgrim's Lament in the Book of Shadows

Upon the road, a pilgrim sighs,
Beneath the weight of weary skies.
Each step a plea, in soft despair,
Seeking solace, a heart laid bare.

In pages worn, his prayers inscribed,
A longing deep, his soul ascribed.
The echoes rise in twilight's breath,
Whispers of hope, defying death.

The shadows dance, a tale untold,
In fervent lines, a truth unfolds.
The path is lonely, the night is long,
Yet faith endures, a steadfast song.

With every heartbeat, the shadows grow,
Tales of sorrow, of joy and woe.
A journey marked on sacred ground,
In every silence, his voice is found.

As dawn arises, his spirit flies,
Into the light, where darkness dies.
A pilgrim's heart, forever lost,
In the book of shadows, we count the cost.

The Silent Hymn of Forgotten Scripts

In inkless whispers, the silence hums,
Forgotten scripts, where the heart succumbs.
Each letter lingers, a breath of dreams,
In shadows cast, the spirit beams.

Echoes of ages, in stillness dwell,
Sacred stories, we weave and tell.
A hymn of loss, yet hope remains,
In silent prayers, the soul contains.

The parchment crumbles, yet faith endures,
Through trials faced, the heart matures.
With every tear, a treasure flows,
In silent hymn, the spirit knows.

Wherever shadows stretch their hand,
There lies a promise, a sacred land.
In forgotten scripts, the wisdom waits,
To guide the lost through heaven's gates.

A silent melody, forever sung,
In every heart, where love is wrung.
The essence lingers, in twilight's shroud,
The silent hymn, both fierce and proud.

Chronicles Lost in Time's Embrace

In the arms of time, we softly fade,
Chronicles lost, and dreams betrayed.
Yet in the stillness, stories lie,
Whispers of fortune, beneath the sky.

Each moment captured, like dew on leaf,
A tapestry woven from joy and grief.
In faded scrolls, the truth remains,
Beneath the weight of history's chains.

The records echo through endless night,
In shadows cast, they find their light.
With every heartbeat, the memories flow,
Chronicles lost, yet still they glow.

From ancient tongues, the lessons rise,
In sacred texts, our spirits prize.
As every grain in sand slips past,
The tales endure, free of their cast.

In time's embrace, we find our place,
Among the echoes of love's sweet grace.
Though chapters fade, the stories bloom,
Chronicles lost, forever loom.

Erased Echoes of the Soul

In the silence of prayer, I find my way,
Whispers of faith guide my weary heart.
Each echo remembered, a timeless ray,
The darkness recedes, lighting paths to impart.

Lost in the shadows, a flicker ignites,
Wounds of the spirit begin to mend.
Grace flows like waters, pure and bright,
The soul's gentle journey finds its end.

In the arms of the light, I am restored,
The past fades away, a fleeting breath.
Hope is a promise, eternally adored,
Through love's compassion, I conquer death.

Every tear fallen, a river of grace,
Carved by the hands of the Divine.
In this sacred space, I find my place,
The echoes of old intertwine with the sign.

Erased but not lost, the soul takes flight,
A dance of redemption, a heavenly sound.
In unity's weave, day turns into night,
In faith's embrace, we are ever bound.

The Faded Pilgrimage

Through valleys of trials, we walk with care,
The map of our hearts, a winding trail.
Each step a prayer, a moment to bare,
In faith's gentle hands, we will not fail.

Mountains of doubt rise high in the sky,
Yet courage ignites as we seek the dawn.
With every breath, we look up and try,
For the light of the heavens calls us on.

Lost in the moments, the past fades away,
The footprints of sorrow, fading to dust.
In the warmth of the sun, in the light of the day,
We rise like the phoenix, in hope we trust.

The journey of souls is woven in grace,
Each challenge a lesson, love's guiding hand.
As pilgrims, we gather, as one we embrace,
The faded whispers of a promised land.

Through trials we wander, yet never alone,
In the book of our lives, each chapter a prayer.
With love as our beacon, the seeds will be sown,
The faded pilgrimage, in faith's tender care.

Remnants of the Celestial

Stardust scattered across the firmament,
Each glimmer a promise, pure and divine.
In the night's embrace, our hearts are bent,
Seeking the sacred, in every design.

The whispers of angels blend with the breeze,
Their songs of comfort wrap around our soul.
In moments of stillness, the spirit agrees,
With the pulse of the cosmos, we feel whole.

Fragments of glory in each fleeting glance,
The echoes of heaven dance wild and free.
In faith's tapestry, we spin our chance,
To connect the divine with our humble plea.

Carved in the silence, an everlasting grace,
The remnants of love in all that we feel.
Under the heavens, we find our space,
In the sacred symphony, our wounds heal.

In the heart of the night, we find our peace,
With the stars as witnesses to life's grand dream.
In celestial arms, all troubles cease,
The remnants of the holy, intricately seam.

Fragments of a Holy Dream

In visions of grace, night blooms like a flower,
Petals of hope grace the garden of minds.
With every prayer whispered, we gather power,
In fragments of light, our purpose unwinds.

Clouds of doubt linger, yet faith lights the dark,
Through valleys of sorrow, we carry the flame.
Each sparkle of insight ignites a new spark,
Awakening spirit to rise without shame.

The echoes of dreams that connect us all,
In whispers of kindness, the heart beats as one.
Through trials and triumphs, we answer the call,
To shine as reflections, where glory is spun.

In the waters of love, we wash our despair,
With grace as our anchor, we learn how to soar.
In fragments of joy, we breathe in the air,
And find in our journey, we are evermore.

United in faith, we chase the holy light,
Each moment a blessing, each day a new stream.
In the tapestry woven with threads shining bright,
We live out our truth in fragments of dream.

Fragments of the Sacred Scroll

In quietude, the whispers dwell,
Ancient words from a sacred shell.
A promise wrapped in twilight's glow,
Each fragment sings, the truth we know.

Under the stars, our hearts aligned,
The echoes of faith, serene and blind.
With every breath, a prayer we weave,
In the tapestry of love, we believe.

Beneath the sky, the spirits call,
In sacred whispers, we rise and fall.
The scroll unravels, a story untold,
In humble hearts, the mysteries unfold.

Through trials faced, in darkness found,
The fragments bind, though we are bound.
In every loss, a lesson gained,
In sacred silence, our souls are trained.

The touch of grace, a guiding light,
In every shadow, we hold on tight.
As we journey forth, hand in hand,
These fragments guide where hope shall stand.

Whispered Verses of the Lost

In the hush of night, a voice appears,
Carried through wind, dissolving fears.
Each whispered verse, a gentle thread,
Stitches our hearts, where angels tread.

Beneath the surface, in silence deep,
The stories linger, the promises keep.
In shadows cast by the moon's soft light,
The lost find solace in sacred sight.

A tapestry woven, lost and found,
With threads of love that circle round.
Each verse a step on a winding way,
Leading the spirit, come what may.

In brokenness, there lies a truth,
Of whispered verses, reclaiming youth.
In every sigh, a hope reborn,
The lost are found at the break of dawn.

Through trials faced, in faith so bold,
These whispered tales need to be told.
In every heart, a burden shared,
In whispered verses, we are repaired.

Shattered Hymns of the Devout

In solemn halls, the hymns take flight,
Echoes of love in the still of night.
Though shattered voices rise from the gloom,
Each note resounds, dispelling doom.

Under the weight of a weary sky,
The devout gather, their spirits nigh.
In broken songs, their truth ignites,
Each shattered hymn brings new insights.

With every tear, a melody flows,
In offerings made, the spirit grows.
The chorus of hearts, a fervent cry,
Through shattered hymns, we learn to fly.

In the ashes, redemption glows,
The devout unfurl where the river flows.
From every fracture, a light breaks through,
With shattered hymns, we're born anew.

Together we stand, hand in hand,
In faith's embrace, a steadfast band.
Through trials faced, we find our way,
With shattered hymns, we choose to stay.

The Dispersed Testament

In sacred words, the truth dispersed,
A testament written, hearts rehearsed.
Across the ages, the voices call,
Binding us gently, embracing all.

In every chapter, stories blend,
Through trials faced, we learn to mend.
The scattered pages, wisdom's grace,
Each testament holds a sacred place.

Through laughter shared and sorrows felt,
In whispered dreams, our spirits melt.
The lessons learned, our guiding star,
In the dispersed testament, we know who we are.

With faith as our anchor, we journey forth,
In every corner, we search for worth.
In the hands of the many, the truth remains,
In the dispersed testament, love sustains.

Together we rise, though distances part,
In the living testament, we play our part.
As pages turn, in the light of day,
In every word, the truth will stay.

Divine Footprints on Faded Folios

In the quiet dusk, a whisper leads,
Footprints trace the paths of old deeds.
Hearts open wide, as truth reveals,
The stories of faith, in hushed appeals.

On brittle pages, ink once flowed,
A sacred journey, where hope glowed.
Lessons of love, in shadows cast,
Echo through ages, forever last.

Through every tear, grace gently pours,
In moments of doubt, the spirit soars.
Wisdom etched in the fabric of time,
Guiding the weary, in rhythm and rhyme.

Each fold and crease, a prayer unsung,
In communion with souls, forever young.
Embrace the silence, let voices blend,
In divine footprints, we transcend.

With every glance, the heart ignites,
In faded folios, we find the lights.
Together we journey, hand in hand,
On sacred pages, we understand.

The Unraveled Manuscript of Existence

A parchment crumbles under fate's weight,
Each line a query, a searching state.
In the margins, hope scribbles dreams,
Of purpose and grace, like flowing streams.

Words intertwine, like paths in the night,
Guiding the lost to the source of light.
In the labyrinth of thought, we aspire,
To grasp the essence, the sacred fire.

Lost in the folds, a truth awaits,
In every heartbeat, the spirit creates.
The manuscript sprawls across endless plains,
Bearing the weight of joy and pains.

With ink of devotion, we pen our fate,
In the uncharted, our souls awake.
The chapter unfolds, in loving embrace,
In the manuscript's heart, we find our place.

Each verse whispers tales of the divine,
Threads of existence in every line.
As pages turn, our spirits soar,
In the unraveled, we seek evermore.

Hidden Light in Shredded Texts

Amidst ancient ruins, a glow ignites,
Hidden truths in the faded sights.
In fragments scattered, the spirit grieves,
Yet through the chaos, the light believes.

Shredded texts like scattered dreams,
Holding the echo of sacred themes.
Each syllable whispers of love and grace,
A divine spark in this earthly space.

Through the rips and tears, the message rings,
In the silence, a melody sings.
Hope intertwines with despair's embrace,
In the hidden light, we trace our place.

Tattered pages, yet stories remain,
Of faith and courage, joy and pain.
In the shadows, the heart finds peace,
As hidden light leads us to release.

Though texts may shatter, the spirit thrives,
In the luminous glow, the heart derives.
Embrace the fragments, let love ignite,
In the shattered, we discover light.

The Void Between Stanzas of Grace

In the silence profound, a pause takes form,
A sacred void, where souls are warm.
Between each stanza, a breath of prayers,
Awakening hope, dispelling cares.

The rhythm of grace, in stillness found,
Hums the melody of love unbound.
In the quiet, we seek to connect,
In every heartbeat, we introspect.

Through gaps of time, our spirits blend,
In the void, we discover a friend.
Whispers of wisdom from ages past,
Emanate softly, in shadows cast.

Every heartbeat a stanza, every sigh,
Echoes the longing to reach the sky.
The void sings songs, ancient and sweet,
Where grace and longing lovingly meet.

In the spaces between, the truth aligns,
In every heartbeat, divinity shines.
Embrace the silence, let it embrace,
In the void of stanzas, we find grace.

The Sacred Silence in Lost Verses

In shadows deep, where whispers lie,
A stillness holds the breath of sighs.
The heart finds peace in sacred glow,
As time weaves tales, both high and low.

Each word a prayer, reach for the stars,
In silence found, we've healed our scars.
The echoes dance in twilight's breath,
Embracing life, defying death.

Beneath the veil of night so clear,
The stars above, our hopes sincere.
With every tear, a story told,
Of love divine, and faith so bold.

In sacred sounds, the lost may hear,
The chorus of the heavens near.
Resounding grace in each refrain,
A symphony of joy and pain.

So linger here, in this embrace,
In every void, there lies a space.
For in the silence, hearts can mend,
The sacred silence knows no end.

Threads of Grace in the Abyss

In depths unknown, where shadows cling,
 The threads of grace begin to sing.
 Each note a promise, softly spun,
  In darkest places, hope is won.

With every step through grief's dark haze,
The light will shine through tangled ways.
  In strains of love, we find our guide,
   Embraced by faith, we shall abide.

The fragile threads, a tapestry,
Connecting souls in harmony.
Through trials faced, our spirits soar,
  In unity, we seek the shore.

Let whispers rise in midnight's air,
Each plea a journey, each dream a prayer.
As angels weave through time and space,
  We're held by grace in every place.

So trust the woven path we tread,
 For in our hearts, the light is spread.
  Threads of grace, in the abyss vast,
Will guide us through, our fears surpassed.

Mysteries Scattered in Celestial Decay

In twilight hours, where secrets dwell,
Mysteries dwell, too deep to tell.
Among the stars that flicker faint,
The silence speaks, a holy saint.

Each shadow holds a tale untold,
In cosmic depths, both new and old.
With every breath of night so wide,
The universe, our hearts abide.

What lies beyond the veils of time?
In sacred spaces, we will climb.
Through veils of dark, the light will break,
Awakening dreams, for hope's sweet sake.

In swirling dust, the stars align,
As hearts ignite, our spirits shine.
In celestial dance, we find our way,
Through mysteries lost in decay.

So gather close, and raise your voice,
In every shadow, we rejoice.
For even in the darkest night,
A spark of faith will shine so bright.

The Hushed Prayers of Broken Pages

In pages worn, where stories sleep,
The hushed prayers stir, bound to keep.
Each tear-stained line, a sacred plea,
In whispered hopes, we long to see.

With ink of sorrow, hearts define,
The beauty found in tales divine.
Through every crack, the light will stream,
A tapestry of hope, we dream.

The broken pages tell our fate,
In every fold, we learn to wait.
For in the space where silence reigns,
The essence of our love remains.

So stitch the fragments, weave them tight,
In every shadow, seek the light.
For even hearts that seem so torn,
Can find the path where love is born.

In hushed prayers, our faith will grow,
Each broken page, a chance to show.
In whispers soft, the truth we find,
In every heart, a love entwined.

Milton Keynes UK
Ingram Content Group UK Ltd.
UKHW021240191124
451300UK00007B/158